Sincerely, Light

A COLLECTION OF POETRY BY
BRITTANY DISALVO

Sincerely, Light

A Lyrical Record of Foraged Observations

Brittany DiSalvo
Gold & Light Publishing

As the moon above the mountain,
as a nest within a tree,
as the rain becomes the river,
so are You, my God, to me.

"There is... a chamber in God himself, into which none can enter but the one, the individual, the peculiar man, — out of which chamber that man has to bring revelation and strength for his brethren. This is that for which he was made — to reveal the secret things of the Father."

— George MacDonald

Table of Contents

Letter to Reader

Several years ago, a thought bloomed in my mind that has been growing ever since. It was my first breath of wonder in a remarkably difficult season, asking: What if everything I am standing in is a love letter signed "Sincerely, Light"? And what if I just haven't lived into the rest of the letter yet?

That question was a lantern that helped me see the "letters" sent my way every day: the birdsong outside my window, the eyes that held my gaze, the rain that brewed above me, and the provisions continually set before me. That question was the light that pulled me through a tunnel of agony to the other side.

To see that was a form of receiving. To convey what I have seen continues to be a tedious form of giving. While the medium of conveyance is secondary, for me it so often emerges through the vehicle of language.

I liken my role as a poet in this world to a tour guide at an archaeological site.

Some things I've been able to dust off more than others, and some are more or less familiar in this present age. The more peculiar things have a way of feeling especially worthy of exposure and examination.

What I want is to walk about the brushed-off land and show you a few things I've found so far. To be sure, I'm not the first to find them, I'm not the only one digging, and I strongly suspect that you may be able to find more than I have. Perhaps the closest I can come to giving you a guided tour is to document my findings. That way, you can navigate the grounds of discovery without me.

Without question, my favorite thing I've found in all my digging is the glowing companion, wonder. May you find her as I have, only more so: triumphant in her arrival, raging in her joy, and humble in her holy inquisition.

May this be a map for the pathless woods of life that leads you to find far more than you could ever seek.

Above all, may this book be a magnifier of Light Himself, who does not change like shifting shadows — no matter how much or little we find of Him.

Sincerely,
Brittany

Sincerely, Light

Little Twig,

I know you do not love the friction of your brother,
but if you keep going with it,
you will find me.

Sincerely,
Light

Waves

If you hold still enough,
you can feel the waves your heart makes
in the channels of your veins,
splashing against the retention walls of your extremities.

Your pleated skirts of skin
were ruffled into signatures at your fingertips,
tailor-made seals along untraceable seams
that resemble the ocean's swelling.

And even the ocean can stand like the mountain,
a statue of churning seas;
rolling hills and rising waters are kin.

Color is the pilgrimage of light;
she traverses galaxies
and humbly bends
to be palatable for the eye,
though she keeps most of her frequencies covered.

The voice that is
rides on warm sheets of velvet
swimming in the air,
like the hand of the wind
that tousles the hair of the meadows.

Flames curl brazenly into the skies,
dancing with the breath of a laughing breeze.

The wave of all waves
ripples through all of existence,
rising the tide that kisses your feet
to bid you come further out into the deep.

What Light Cannot but Tell

The mount is sonnet laden
with precise, artful design.
The dust of earth, the breath
of wind and water each entwine.

The measure of the beauty
etched into the mountain's crown
weaves with rooted wisdom
and the company of clouds.

Their linkages of brilliance
binding lyrically therein
form firm and fragile architectures
that whisper what whispered them.

The unencumbered land
arrays a wild elegance
elaborated by a tongue
of holy eloquence.

Gathered waters, in their rest,
reflect the sky's expanse,
echoing the vast refrain
that quells and re-enchants.

We are a soliloquy,
a musing rich with prose,
scribed with ageless wisdom
by benevolence aglow.

We stand within a living poem,
ever does it spell
what words could never wrap around,
what light cannot but tell.

Conversations

The night is a question
and the dew is its answer.

The song of the sparrow is an invitation
to which the wind whistles back.

Sun rays are brazen exclamations
with which water can only gently agree.

Sagging clouds pelt persuasion upon
the mountain that will not change its mind,

yet the coastal cliffs soften
toward the faithful jostling of water.

Galaxies and angels ache for the unspeakable,
while you and I are something God is saying.

Constellate

What are we
beneath the skies?
What do we spell
to open eyes
that read us here below?

We cluster
and reform,
we gather
and
disband.

We sow the sun,
we reap the stars,
and who can see
the stories that we are?

The legends of the sky
speak in dialects of light,
fluent and affluent
in the bond that breathed them there.

When the fault lines of

disconnect

rumble here below,

in my banishment,
or wandering,
or forerunning,
behold:

Bright is the bend in the arm of the king
when I am the stone shot out of the sling.
Not the whole of the scene but a speck in the frame;
not the crown of the king but a sign of his reign.

Oh my soul,
zoom out.

Unphased

The moon is the face of love
that I see, more or less,
depending on the day.
The half has not been shown us
but the waters meet their shores.

The tide is the fruit of the light,
rolling out and bringing in
essence from the deep.

Lunar pull
and human eyes
wax and wane in kind,
and the waters meet their shores.

Dovetail

The wind of the skies
holds harmony in her whispers.

Her overstory can symphonize
every dissonance of us
and weave our laments
into songs of ascent.

Sovereign overtones
scatter like rose petals in procession,
red as blood and detached
as the moon from the earth,
pulling us toward the shores
that sway with the weight of light.

The waters that rose over the heads
of mountains and men
baptize broken stories into songs.

There is newness to be found
like the olive branch that crowned receding waters.
And we can recede,
and we can receive the same.

Tonewood

Hollow rooms resound with light and tone.
The timbre of the timber
swirls within its song-struck home.

The wood floors and swinging doors
are lives laid down and raised anew,
ever telling something true;
they're quills.

Harvested tonewood
rests where its home would resound
with the key of be,
and the key of see.

The death and life of well-wrought beams
are now and ever holding me
in suspense or suspension,
melodic in tension.

The creak of doors and shining floors
harmonize with bending boughs;
their weathered bark is the womb of precious wood.

Logs gutted hollow can sing as the swallow
that carries the weight of a voice,

emptied therein for the sound of a wind
to fill and ring out from the void.

The strength of the trees
and the light of their leaves hold song:
birds now, cellos later.

They are lampstands of wisdom, chambers of sound,
forested pillars that drum with the pulse of the ground.

Lightward they bend,
beams of shade from beams of sun,
and blessed are the emptied ones.
Be still.

Fire by Night

Press the olive, light the lamp.

Find the tree in the table

and the table in the tree

whose branches bow

heavy with oil

to broaden their shade,

turning the light of day

into the fire of night.

Miles Between Trees

Parabolic roots are knit under varicose floors,
making the skin of the forest
bulge with the strength of connection.

They weave like my father's love
that stretches for miles.

And there are miles between trees, miles.
There are miles within all the veins of their leaves,
and miles of life above and beneath.

Arborescence

Oaks don't bend,
willows bow,
and junipers dig deep.

Their darker rings are still
the work of light.

Their heartwood rests within
cathedrals of rising sweetness.

Legacy ripples out like water
scattering, scattering
into a crown of rings.

Their open hands
extend vibrant pearls
wrought faithfully
from their cores.

Each is born out
of what tells
the spring to spring,
the seed to fall
and rise again.

The water in the mud
washes the feet of trees
and the eyes of men

that they may stand, still,
holding and beholding the sun.

Watershed

You told me that you know
the paths I've tread
in avoidance.

I stomped my feet onto unbending desert ground
and such was I.
I told you that your patience felt like neglect.
You told me that you know

how the desert reflects
the sun above,
and the life behind!

I thought I loved you more
back when I knew you less.
But I think I was mistaken,
and you know how

I couldn't bear to face
and face
and face again
how much I love you so
conditionally.

But water pooled into the places I tread —
and pulled me into places I still haven't said —
while you hold every desert within a watershed.

Down With the Sun

I found your narrow mountain road
and walked with you
to the edge of your final days.

It rolled into a storm of a descent,
brief and electrifying
as the static between dark clouds.

The road wound down
and jetted out over cavernous depths.

You tread knowingly, helplessly,
unraveling between your future and your past.

We trekked to the sea of your final voyage.
I can still feel the gravel crunching under my feet.
Every step marked the road like it marked me
as we wound down, down, down with the sun
to dignity lost and dignity won.

You carried a load.
Your bondage, your freedoms,
your child, your need of
smoke and high gravity,
regret and audacity

to break out of prison,
twice.

I can't forget the way
your graying eyes thanked mine
as we drew nearer to the waters
that had drawn you all that time.

Your fragility tenderized me into thin places
where love blurred and cured my vision.
My eyes were branded
by your vital organs next to you
hung by thin and yellowed threads
that frayed into your frame.
You writhed with life —
that was the last I saw of you.

I still don't know if you died alone.
My heart stands still
when I go past your home
on the other side of Spring.

I was shaped — and surprised —
by your strength to descend,
to face waters as cold and as clear as our end —
the same waters that mirror what honor can mend.

Deciduous

Delighted branch, I was.
Grafted into soil and anchored to stand
where I was sentenced to the toil of stillness.

Yes — I shed my covering before winter came.
Strange — to greet the cold in nakedness.
But every part of me
so desperately needed
the touch of light in waning days.

The knife edge of that careless wind
is sweeter to me than dead remains.
What has fallen from my grasp
now nourishes my roots.

Irretrievable.
Dissolving.
Sown.

But I won't live to see it grown.
My pearls of joy cast down, down.
I had no say.

I held fruit — sometimes.
For a little bit. Barely.

It hung from my skeletal hands,
frail umbilical cords of mighty life.
And just when it was at its best,
it fell.
Or was ripped from my arms
by hands that did not grow it,
did not know it.

All my growing led to grieving.
And I will never hold again
what I was sure was mine.

Do not call me benevolent;
I am bereaved.

I rest.
I cultivate.
I hold.
I treasure.
And I release.

Over
and over
and over again.

I am chained to theft and decay
until the earth releases me.

Colonel

You face the sun
because
your life depends on it.

You hold your ground
and kiss the sky
that leaves you in the dark.

And, when light has borne
seeds in your head,
you bow —

a curtsy
at your repertoire's end,
where soon you will cast
no shadow.

Firelight

You're a watchman, aren't you?
There is goodness in feeling you burn with unease
on my behalf
as you renovate what should have been honored
and fire what should not have been trusted.

You're a mighty asset.
Late have I noticed you,
little have I heeded you.
You're a whipping wind at the door of my lips,
knocking to rush through my airways,
deepen my breaths,
and free my lungs for richer laughter.

You rage fire but clear the air
so I don't choke on second-hand hope
or build with brittle elements.

You're a humble peacemaker
in a ruffian's clothes.
You are sometimes mistaken for threat, or power,
and your offerings are easily ignored
or hoarded beyond their ripeness.

You are not power, you only signify it;
like the thunder that announces lightning's strike.

You work as a precursor, eager to leave.
You seem to not want to linger
and to not like to be ignored.
You like sprints, not marathons,
but you will go every distance required.
The first bricks on the pathways to freedom
are humbly laid by you.

You mingle wind and flame,
imparting how to drive pegs through wicked temples,
and overturn tables of false profit,
and arrange bouquets of resolve from foraged observations.

You're a sprout in healing's spring,
a forerunner, a signifier that healing can come.
But I can't swallow you down on an empty stomach,
I need to take you in with the hope of joy you prepare.

You bellow that the mercy that triumphs over
judgment does not make justice obsolete.
Your table is set for both to come
in full array, side by side, neither nullifying the other.

I waited too long to be still with you.
You have so much to say,
and I see now that you can help me
find my voice where I have swallowed it.

We want the same thing at our cores.
You've never actually worked against me.

Tell me what I've never heeded.
Because now, like a strong kiss,
full faced toward your passion,
I will take in the breath of your mouth.

Budding Blaze,

Why didn't you tell me how much this would burn,
and how we would be less of whatever we were?

Appalled,
The Ashes of Little Twig

Heartspun

Hold reverence for story.
It was all imagined:

Heartspun characters emerging in

> *loyalty*
> > *and war,*
>
> *play*
> > *and suspense,*
>
> *catastrophe*
> > *and resolve.*

We — we were all imagined.

> *And here*
> > *we are*
> > > *for now.*

Away

How can the harvest feel like a thief?

What do I make
of tall stalks cut down to their roots
and taken from where I tended them?

Sly is the fox that spoils the vineyard;
true are the hands that harvest the fruit.

Is this the giver or the thief?
Is this of honor or of grief?

My fields, now bare in due season,
urge me to discern the times.

Is this the giver or the thief?

Where is the table for all my starving senses?
Who will savor—or savage—what I've grown?
There's nothing in the field but a damned Tree.

Fox & Shadow

Here at the harvest I see through my tears
the fruit that my labor has rendered:

I was the locust who stole all those years,
and I was the fox in the vineyard.

But you were the kindness that sent forth the rain
in the cover of shadow and cloud,

and you'll be the mountain that stretches your shade
across the fields fallow and plowed.

Whether I squander my days that are numbered
or toil until they are done,

You set a table that nothing could plunder
to which I may faithfully come.

My Good

I'm so glad
You know
what I'm forgetting,
and all I cannot see.

The horizons my eyes find
are near enough to touch.

But You are nearer,
and touching Your nearness
opens me to Your vastness.

My Lord, where are You not?

Rise

I reach for your face
with the light of mine
every morning.

I cover you
before you open your eyes,
and there is bread.

I ache
for your gaze,
and there is bread.

You stir
with fading slumber,
finding crumbs around your eyes.

They fall
when faced with vision
and my burning question rises:

Will the sleeping facets
of your diamond eyes
be wakened
to the uncharted hues of who
I am?

Kindred

If your voice
sounds like water
and deep calls out to deep
and you told the storms to cease —
did the waves hear mighty waters
before they sighed into that stillness?

For Givenness

I want to know the magnetism
of how water is held together.

I want to see the shape
of the wind before it gives itself to the sea.

I want to live like the shores
of sand and stone, giving and being given

like the rain that knows nothing
of reluctance.

Navel

Tomatoes have belly buttons
and I was harvested in winter,
a human cut from that green cord, and,
strange —

that we are a fruit that grows
after being plucked.

For the Mirror

You were born
of the will of the Spirit,
dreamed up
by His wisdom and love.
You were formed
in a womb made to nurture,
and brought forth
in both water and blood.

You were made
not from need of fulfillment.
You were made
not for function alone.
You were born
from the beauty of Jesus,
and you're here
to make sweeter His home.

Rhodes

Wild grow the woods that we'll never ever see,
hidden far away from the edges of the seas.
Wildly you've grown, yet you've never been unseen,
weaving in the dark, shouldering a dream.

Strong be the wind that pulls you to risk.
Clear be your eyes through the fog, in the mist.
Soft be the shores of endeavors unseen.
Timely be the blooms in your heart of evergreen.

Tall be the pine that adorns you with shade.
Full be its limbs with the needles it made.
Gold be the thread weaving hope into view.
Lush be the crown that flowers over you.

Long be the dance of the flame in your eyes.
Crushed underfoot be the arrow that flies.
Long live the laugh from the heart that is true.
Deeper grow the love that awakens in you.

So keep growing wild like the iris in bloom.
Keep holding light like the dust on the moon.
Keep all your whimsy and your wisdom will bloom.
Keep keeping us, and let us keep you.

Eclipsed

I see a strand, a string of thoughts that flow freest unspoken,
link truest unbroken.
It's Love —
a free-flow
of what the receiver may never know — on earth.
That which I live in, I behold.
But not to dissect,
which would in fact infect
my joy with death.
So instead I breathe deep
and rest.

It's rest and resistance
as I stand as one silent,
tried a saint or a tyrant —
but not with blood.
Yet stilled I stand as one guiltless within,
by another without sin.
I'm his friend and I sit at His table.
That ball and that chain were cast off and disabled for good,
for me, and for him, though it stood
like the cedars of immeasurable meters.
But it was broken by the word that was spoken into life
and broken thus unto death
while the created held their breath

in darkness, mark this:
To be overcome by light
though they mourned in the silence of night.

Who will now see the light in the trees,
the water in the leaves from the source to which all things
return?
It burns.

And I hang my head in rest, a kind of death,
as I look to the west
gazing on to the reverse of dawn
in search of light and I hear the stars say,

"It is not here."
And the dawn, "It is risen."

Behind me!
Surprising!
Now rising where I never thought to look
because I mistook earth's decrescendo for hope's dismissal.
But! The darkness is hope's very stage!
Not freedom's cage, just trust engaged.

And the free ones understand, look on, and clap their hands
while the others march callous, masqueraders,
as they try and they try to compose

what the free man knows
was only meant to be enjoyed!
A symphony
for the religiously
unemployed

who move their feet to the Beat that was
from the beginning
synchronized with the heartbeat and unending:

Love.
Behold, love.

Arrowhead

Love is a weapon of holy war.
It's the very flame of God,
and did I even know this before now?
Not that, but how He delights in me?
I used to just read the sheet music
but now I hear Him sing over me.
And it's the sweetest thing,
a mighty pendulum swing
that came to toss and upheave
every one of my fables
because I could reason with being replaceable!
And not just because I survived Roe vs. Wade, either.
This Love is alive and I house His heartbeat.
We say there's no place like home,
He says there's no place like me.
I'm a piece of His heart,
an intricate part,
a flame He will breathe on
to unmake the dark
because love
never
fails.

Ever.

Promise Comes in Waves

Rivers rush down mountains at this very moment,
while vital rivers stream from the hearts of all who breathe.

The sun casts a beaming gaze upon its string of pearls.
The delighted eyes of a mother beam the same.

The eagle swims in the channels of the sky,
and belonging known makes the heart soar with joy.

Rainbows crown the ground beneath our feet
and promise comes in waves of light
that are only vivified after storms.

Why Do You Tremble?

Why do you tremble in the land of your victory?
Where is your spoil and who is your king?

Who is your king?

What is this mountain that towers above you?
Whose hands are able to turn it to dust?

Who is your king?

Who has gone before you
and leveled every mountain?
Behold the dust beneath you,
the hills became a plain.

Who is your king?
Who is your king?

Storehouses

Storehouses walk upon the earth.
Perhaps you are near one now
and surely you are one now,
you breathing cellar,
aging with the blood-red wine of life.

Look longer in the faces of your neighbors; this is grain.
Memorize the stories in their eyes; they are wine,
and let them see what hope and woe are pressing out of you.

Pour it out like water from the stone.
Harvest from the field that love has sown.
Feed upon what faithfulness has grown.
Drink the cup of honor til it seeps into your bones;
all it needs is a humble home.

Scatter your stores like thunder across barren fields,
just as the cloud-crashed song drums its echoes
into the pores of the earth.
Let your love be a storm over thirsty ground,
a light pulsing through the veins of darkened skies.

Oh, Sister

How precious to wash His feet with your tears
as He renders you open-hearted,
while He gathers stray cords of love
through the years
to continue what He started.

Add shattered ones to your dwelling
and watch Him render this family whole.
This phenomenon comes with wonders
you would not believe even if you were told.

Look at children of nations and watch
and be utterly amazed.
Look at their faces, see the gleam of His eye
beaming love into you through their gaze.

The Jerusalem from above is free
and this is our mother.
Your open heart is His open door
to turn strangers into brothers.

So gather your best,
even your dreams from His chest,

to set as jewels into His crown.
Listen again and you'll find Him a friend
who honors your trust with new ground.

I see heaven's army revering
the impact of your surrender.
You may not know it, but one yes from you
is worth a thousand for what it renders.

You know, you never needed
to fear the serpent you heeded
and I'll tell you a secret now:
When you shot in the dark
with your dreams shed apart
your arrows hit him straight in the heart.

He writhed and recoiled
but you will gather the spoil
to carry away as a light to the dark,
setting the table
with lampstands and angels
and oil wrung out of your scars.

Please don't despise
the pain that opened your eyes
and broke open your heart of alabaster.

Come home to His wounds,
they're your own healing rooms
where He wires you to bleed out compassion.

The arrows in your side
can all be chiseled into keys,
one by one unlocking His house
and setting your own heart free.
Darkness shudders at the light in your eyes
even when you're not at your best.
Remember the morsels of bread that fed thousands
and sister, be at rest.

Speak to This Mountain

Bless the valley of vision
for the day of decision
and dig till you've opened a well.
What you draw from this fountain
you'll speak to the mountain
and crumble the structures of hell.

May the hours of testing
find your heart resting
assured that he works to one joy.
May morning's great fire
draw you up higher
to see what cannot return void.

No weapon will prosper
against what you've fostered
in spirit or labored in love.
No fortress could shield
or shadow conceal
what light has conceived from above.

The sun rays rain down,
pouring light to the ground;

the prismatic promise comes through
shoots that spring up
by the fountain you dug
and you are the mountain it moves.

Emerge from your fearing
and you'll come to a clearing
where a seed is entrusted to you.
Let your heart be the soil
for the seed to uncoil
for it has much to breathe into you.

May your posture of holding
beget an unfolding
of all that was hid in the seed.
Keep it watered with tears
and untouched by all fear
in the light dancing down through the Tree.

Keep your ear to the ground
for heaven come down,
but remember the way of the cross.
The God-seed of love
uncoiled in blood
and was sown in a garden tomb plot.

The tomb of the garden
is the womb of the Artist,
bulging with raw mystery.
Behold, it is true!
He makes everything new,
even murder, betrayal, and greed.

Christ is the seed of Jerusalem's spring,
the turn of all seasons commenced.
Kingdom won't just come down,
it bursts out of the ground
with a life even death ushers in.

Ash,

I made you free from everything but the wind.
Are you flying yet?

Warmly,
Your Light

Honor To Whom Honor

This book is an outworking of gratitude for the support of several individuals that I cannot help but mention. Receiving a generous amount of encouragement, attention to detail, and financial backing is as baffling as it is catalyzing.

My Lord, my strength, I love You. You saved the best wine for last.

Preston, thank you forever for what you've built in Gold & Light. Your eagerness and ability to serve this project was outdone only by your continual distinction between what I create and who I am. Thank you for the unwavering celebration. The joy of the Lord is surely your strength.

Valina, I will echo the psalmist to say, "You saw my unformed substance." Thank you for listening so intently to my high and varied hopes for the cover and turning it into something that is both stunning and rich with meaning.

Blake, working with you was a blast. Your ability to question when it's time to question and celebrate when it's time to celebrate is a rare art form. You did it with a sharp precision and warmth of wisdom that I am richer for. I am certain that I would only love half of these poems half as much without your feedback!

Jensen, thank you for being so generous with your time and intellect in contributing to the strength of these poems. Your attention to the poetic details of life and the written word is unmatched. I retain, enjoy, and revere the things you have to say.

To the 45 people who supported the fundraiser that brought this book to life: Thank you, from the bottom of my heart. You gave above and beyond what I asked for and cheered me on in ways I'll never forget. You are so much of the reason you are holding this book in your hands.

To the ones who inspired some of the poems in this collection: You are the prisms that have shone an unforgettable light. You and your lives are better than anything I could say, while still demanding poetic attention. Dad, Mom, Katyann. Lincoln, Shannon, Zach. Rachel, Jasper, Spencer. Joanna, Kelly, Kameri. Christine, Mike, Jyoti. Rebecca.

And to you, the reader: Of all the places your attention could be given, you have turned it here, and I thank you for that. May you receive much.

About the Author

Brittany DiSalvo has been teaching, writing, and sharing poetry for nearly two decades.

Since 2018, she has facilitated writing groups within juvenile facilities, non-profit headquarters, and a vast array of living rooms. She is a Montessori educator who especially adores fanning the flame of wonder within children in her classroom.

Brittany is convinced that the best things she'll ever write are letters to those she loves. She currently resides in Winston-Salem, North Carolina, the soil that has exponentially grown her lifelong fascination with trees.

For more information on Brittany DiSalvo, visit:
www.brittanydisalvo.com

To discover more from Gold & Light Publishing, visit:
www.goldandlightpublishing.com

CPSIA information can be obtained
at www.ICGtesting.com
Printed in the USA
BVHW040314190423
662584BV00003B/83